Kememu.
Move Mountains!
Through <u>Christ</u>!

♡ Andrea Dougherty

Moving Mountains

A story of God's Love and Healing as seen by
Stage 4 Colon Cancer Survivor and Fighter

Written by

Andrea Dougherty

Book Cover illustration by

Andrea Dougherty

First Printing: 2017

ISBN 978-1-365-96755-9

For Erika. Live in the Moment, Dear.

For Akiko.

For Penny, and the color yellow.

For Joe.

For Berta and her blue nails.

Preface

I would like to first acknowledge and introduce some of the special little ones in my life. These kids were on my heart and mind well before I was diagnosed with cancer. They have been in my prayers and the prayers of many others. We have seen God work miracles work through them. They have dealt with suffering, pain, and challenges very early in life. Some things they have in common are that they are joyful. They are determined. They are amazing. They are strong.

They are my Heroes.

Gracie and Maeci

Gracie, also known as Amazing Grace, is 11 years old. At the age of 3, she was diagnosed with a Grade ll Oligoastrocytoma Brain Tumor. She has endured three brain surgeries, two years of chemo, and a countless number of other treatments and scans. All the while she was playing softball, volleyball, and going to school, and just being a totally amazing kid! She and Maeci met while in treatment at Riley, and have been the best of friends since. Gracie continues to have scans every six months.

Maeci is 17. When she was just ten years old, she was diagnosed with State 4 Hodgkin's Lymphoma. She endured seven months of harsh treatment. Maeci has been cancer-free for six years and is scanned regularly. She will be graduating from high school next year.

Gracie and Maeci together have granted *18 wishes* for other children going through cancer treatment through the Make a Wish Foundation. They have raised *$100,000* in five years and were awarded the *Red Cross Humanitarian Award in 2013* and the *Chris Greicus Society of Hope Award in 2017.* These two girls have taught me and many others so many things. I have thought of them many times throughout my treatment. The things they have endured. The role models they are. These are big shoes for me to fill. Little feet, but such big shoes!

Stephanie

Stephanie was born with a medical condition known as Methylmalonic Acidemia. This is a metabolic disorder where the enzyme in the liver is defective. It causes the inability to properly digest proteins, which in turn leads to a buildup of a toxic level of acid in the blood. The acid took her hearing and damaged her eyesight, as well as her liver and kidneys. She had a feeding tube placed when she was very young and has been on a very monitored diet. Even so, the damage done to her liver and kidneys over the years caused her to require a life-saving transplant, which she was approved for in 2016. Stephanie and family traveled to Pennsylvania for her liver and kidney transplant. The surgery was extremely difficult.

Finally, Stephanie came home and is doing well. Her transplant did not cure her condition, but it has set back the clock on the damage done to her organs. She is able to enjoy eating, and is able to add some proteins to her diet with her new liver functioning properly. She has started enjoying cheeseburgers, especially the Big Mac. Stephanie has reminded me that it's fun to play and pretend. We love to play babies together. She also taught me how to knit! Stephanie doesn't let her illness stop her from enjoying life! She has performed in many musicals, and has a great sense of humor. She loves to make up songs and laugh and play. Stephanie is 22 years old and will be graduating from high school this year. She has blessed me and many others with her joyful personality and sweet smile.

Jackson

Jack is my nephew, my 'best boy ever'. He was born with Dandy Walker Syndrome. This was discovered when my sister was pregnant with him. We had never heard of Dandy Walker. The Dandy Walker Malformation is a rare congenital defect that involves the cerebellum and fourth ventricle in the brain. It affects development and causes hydrocephalus. Many people were praying for Jack before he was even born. My sister said the prayers were so strong she could feel them hitting her, like a wave of calmness. She knew that no matter what Jack's limitations would be, that he would be perfect. When Jack was just 7 months old, he had surgery to place a shunt in the ventricle in the back of his brain. The shunt allows Jack to function normally. It saved his life. The extra fluid drains into his abdomen and is absorbed by his body.

Jack is very intelligent. He loves to learn new things. He says that his shunt helps him to be so smart. He is very determined, and was even given an award for his determination in school. This kid is so special to me and to so many others. He is not only a little genius, but is also very good at sports, in school, and at his new hobbies of bottle flipping and doing tricks with his fidget spinners. Jack is truly a miracle boy. Thank you, sweet Jesus.

Kendall

This remarkable little girl has my heart. She was born with Neurofibromatosis. This is a genetic condition where tumors grow on the nerve endings throughout her body. She was diagnosed as an infant. She has endured surgeries for bladder and tumor removal, and chemo when her tumors have turned cancerous. She has tumors lining her abdomen, pelvis and spine. She has endured pain that none of us will ever understand. Kendall is now six years old and just completed a remarkable year of kindergarten!

When she was a baby this seemed like an unattainable goal. She has touched the hearts of many. She does tricks in her wheelchair and likes to race across the living room with her brothers and anyone who will chase her.

She loves to play Littlest Pet Shop and Shopkins. Kendall knows joy. She knows love. She also knows pain. I thought of Kendall many times as I endured pain. Kendall once asked me if her legs will work in heaven, to which I answered, "Of course! Everything on our body works in heaven, and we don't have any pain!" She smiled.

This little girl has taught me so much about being joyful. Joyful through any trial. We can all learn a lot from Kendall and these other children.

One of the biggest things we can learn from children is to have childlike faith. Children are a lot wiser in some ways than adults. They take things at face value. They believe. They tell the truth, most of the time! We can learn so much from little ones.

And as little Gracie has taught us all, **"God's Got It!"**

Moving Mountains

Chapter 1

Feb 1, 2015 was a fun day. I remember it well. The super bowl was on, so I had invited some family over for a get together. I have always loved parties and family gatherings, so any occasion calls for some food and lots of family and friends. There were 12 of us sitting on what I call my comfy couch. A sectional, soft and inviting, old and beat up, but so wonderful. But I just couldn't get comfortable. Even comfy couch seemed to hurt my sides and back. The food smelled amazing, though I could not stand the thought of eating it. For months, I had felt this way. Hungry, but full. It seemed I was gaining weight but hardly eating anything. I remember talking to my sister that night, telling her to feel how tight my stomach was. It felt as if I was pregnant, although I had been dieting and exercising. I told her, "I think I need to go the ER or something. This just isn't right."

I had been seeing a doctor, a wonderful doctor who would end up saving my life just 12 days later. However, my symptoms of the past year had been dismissed. I was too young to have this kind of cancer. I was having pain because of my fibroids. I was told no, it wasn't a good idea to have this test or that test as they are not conclusive. Let's just plan to take these fibroids out, he said. Sometimes they even go away with menopause. Did I want to wait?

Feb 2, 2015. This cannot wait another day. My husband was home from work, so I asked him to take me to the ER. The pain was worse today. It seemed like my stomach was even bigger. How was this possible when the day before I had only eaten some spinach dip, two crackers and a bite of a chicken wing?! Off to the ER we went.

The ER was full. We waited a long while and were lucky to get a private room, as patients were lining the hallways, some in beds, some in wheelchairs. I received some amazing medicine for pain and found myself almost comfortable. While Dave and I were waiting, we were watching a small TV playing Criminal Minds. We watched about 5 episodes that afternoon while we were there. I was so happy to hear they were going to give me a CT scan! Finally, I would find out what was causing this pain and I would hopefully get some kind of relief! After hours of waiting, they came to get me. A kind nurse rolled me through the hallways that were filled with sick and hurting people. Too many patients, not enough rooms. I was so glad for my private room and couldn't wait to get back in it. The scan didn't take long, and I was wheeled back to the room where I had comfort.

Not even fifteen minutes after being returned to my room, the doctor came in. The look on his face told me that he had seen something. He said to me, "Your scan shows a mass in your abdomen." I was aware of the fibroid on my uterus. I explained to him that the doctor I had been seeing for the past year had told me of the fibroid, and attributed all of my symptoms to that. To which he replied, "No, we also see the fibroid. There is an additional mass, on your left ovary, measuring about 12cm." He continued, "You need to be seen immediately. The nurses are on the phone now with Simon Cancer Center to schedule you an appointment. They are hoping to get you in tomorrow."

Cancer???! Did he just say CANCER CENTER???!

I felt my heart fall a little bit. Did my heart actually fall out of the place it is usually located in? I don't think I have felt this happen before. I didn't ask many questions. I said ok. Dave had many questions, but I didn't have the answers. We looked at the TV, still playing Criminal Minds. The doctor came back in with the information on my appointment the next day.

We went home. I still didn't feel well, so I was on the couch most of the evening. The girls came home from school. They brought joy into the house with them. I was terrified for what may be ahead, but today I was at home, the girls were happy and healthy, and comfy couch felt pretty good. Tomorrow would come soon enough.

Matthew 6:34 So don't worry about tomorrow, for tomorrow will bring its own worries. Today's trouble is enough for today.

Chapter 2

February 4, 2015. The drive to the Cancer Center was quiet. Dave had taken the day off work to go with me. We waited to see the doctor in a large waiting area. As we were waiting, we noticed the other patients. A woman in her 40's, reading a book. She was bald. She was also very beautiful. An older man, in a wheelchair. Very thin. So thin. He smiled at me. Another woman sitting and waiting. It was obvious she didn't feel well. I noticed her skin was an odd color, almost gray. I didn't know much about cancer at this time. There was no way I could understand how sick this woman felt. I didn't know that her entire body ached and even as she sat there, she was feeling pain. I am an expert now. Knowledge is power. I should rephrase that. I know a lot about cancer now. I am not an expert. There is too much to know. Cancer is so complex. Cancer is smart. Cancer is painful. It is exhausting. It is scary. Cancer is a beast. I do know that.

The doctor that I spoke with at the Cancer Center is not the doctor I decided to have surgery with, but he is the one who told me that this was likely cancer. Again, that word. *Cancer.* My heart fell from its normal placement in my chest again. As we talked about the details of surgery and recovery, my mind drifted to my daughters. The doctor was talking, but I wasn't really listening. All I could think of was my girls. *I cannot leave my girls. They need me. It is always me and them.* Cancer. *Please don't be cancer. I need to live for my girls.*

I was sent to get more bloodwork. It was me and a nurse in a small room. She asked how I was doing, and I told her of the events of today and yesterday. Tears welled up in her eyes. She asked if she could pray for me. She prayed over me and I felt peace. As I opened my eyes, I saw a sign on the wall in her little room. This is what it said.

Do not tell God about your big problems.

Tell your problems about your BIG GOD.

I knew when I saw this sign that God would see me through this. God is bigger. Meeting this nurse and seeing this sign in her office was no accident. God is bigger. Bigger than cancer, bigger than my fear, bigger than any mountain that is before me. I knew from this moment that God would be with me. I could almost hear him saying, 'Trust Me.' But it was more like a feeling than a voice.

The day at the cancer center was exhausting. It felt wonderful to be home. The next nine days were a blur of pain, decisions, fear, and prayer. A surgery. They would remove the mass, do a biopsy, determine if it is cancerous, and go from there. I would not know the results or my diagnosis until I would awaken from surgery. One of the hardest things to do at this time was to tell my family the news and of the upcoming surgery. My family is amazing, and God has surrounded me with such wonderful friends, many of whom are like family also. He knew of the battle that was ahead, and surrounded me with a great army to help me fight.

Just a small part of my family pictured here. This was in Florida the year before my cancer diagnosis.
I had been having symptoms this entire year.

Chapter 3

I was lucky to grow up in a loving home with my Mom, Dad, younger sister and brother. My childhood is full of wonderful memories of family get togethers, lots of food, and all my cousins at grandma's house. I am blessed with many wonderful aunts, uncles, cousins and family, as my Dad has nine brothers and sisters and my Mom has five sisters and two brothers. We used to joke that we couldn't go anywhere without running into a cousin or a cousin's cousin. We took fun trips and always had an extra kid or three. My family did not regularly go to church, nor was I well versed in the Bible, but Mom and Dad made sure we knew that God loved us, and that He was real. Occasionally we would attend the little white church that my dad grew up in. My grandma was the piano player and my great aunt was the organist. Oh, how I love that little white church! I went to summer church camp with my aunt and uncle a couple of times. My uncle was a Baptist preacher, and I just loved going to camp and church with them. These are great memories of my childhood. There are so many.

This was the extent of my knowledge of God growing up. However, I always felt the presence of God. I always felt Him, knocking at the door of my heart. Several times I know He has even sent Angels to save me and my family. No matter what I was doing, how busy I was, how much I thought I was in control, He was always there, knocking.

Revelation 3:20 Here I am! I stand at the door and knock. If anyone hears my voice and opens the door, I will come in and eat with that person, and they with me.

There were times when the Lord was calling to me. Times when

He saved me. I have always felt His presence, known that He was protecting me, but I continued to push Him away. When I was younger, the thought of God scared me too much to pursue the information. The thought of living FOREVER was too much too think about.

I remember lying in bed at night, about 12 years old or so, wide awake, with that thought haunting me. What in the world would I do for FOREVER?! That was just too long and too scary, so I tried not to think about it. I tried not to think about God, who was calling to me. Years later, in my early twenties, I was too busy having fun. Drinking, partying, doing what I wanted to do, dating this guy and that guy. I didn't have time for God, but I knew I wanted to get with Him later. He continued to knock at the door of my heart. Through years of darkness and bad decisions, God was still there. Calling to me, loving me, with open arms, knocking on the door of my heart.

I did not understand this kind of love at the time, but now I do. Having children changed my way of thinking. Becoming a mom saved my life. I didn't understand this kind of love until I was in my thirties. God loves us as we love our children. He loves us no matter what. And the crazy thing is, that He loves us even MORE than we love our children. MORE than we are even capable of loving. This is something that took me a lifetime to understand, and something that I try to share.

There is nothing you can do to make God love you any more or any less. He just does. He just IS. You cannot earn your way to Heaven or earn God's love. He just gives it. You only have to accept it. Why did it take me so long to understand this? God didn't love me because of who I am, but because of who He is!

Chapter 4

How do I tell my girls? What do I say? How will they handle this, when I can barely handle it myself? How can I tell them I will be okay when I'm so afraid that I'm not going to be? I have always been honest with them about everything. All these questions and more were going through my mind the days after the trip to the ER as I waited for surgery. Each day, my stomach was swelling more and more, to the point that I could hardly breathe. I had to tell them something.

It had always been me and my girls. Although I am married to their father, it is always just me and the girls. Sporting events, family get-togethers, musical performances, dinners at home, always just me and the girls, and our wonderful extended family and friends. Their father is a good man, and is a hard worker, but is not typically present in our daily activities. *How could I leave my girls?* My biggest fear was leaving them on this earth, without me. It was also their biggest fear. Although this fear still haunts them, as I am still fighting this cancer, it is something we have learned to live with.

When I could not handle these thoughts on my own, my wonderful friends who are also like spiritual mentors to me, would remind me of this important lesson I learned. God loves me. He loves my girls. He loves them even more than I love them! Knowing that He loves them this much, I need not worry about who would take care of them if I would leave this earth while they were still young. God knows them and loves them and knows what is best for them even more than I do. I learned to trust God for His Will to be done in our lives. If He would take me out of this body, then He would provide for them. I trust God with them.

After all, they are not really mine, they are HIS. This has been the worst kind of suffering that cancer can cause. Even the pain is not as bad as the thought of leaving my girls.

I know that Heaven awaits me when I go, and what a glorious day that will be. But my hope is that God allows me much more time here. I'm not done here on earth. I have much more to do.

Olivia was 14, a freshman in high school. When she came in from school, I asked her to come and sit with me. Our hearts are connected, and she sensed that something was wrong. I told her, "Olivia they found something in my stomach that is not supposed to be there." Her eyes were filled with sadness and fear. She asked if it was cancer. I told her they didn't know yet if it was cancer or not, they only knew that it had to come out and then we would know more. She cried. I cried. We held each other. She asked me if I might die. I said, "No way! Do you know how strong I am?" She said yes. I told her I was one tough mama and I was going to be fine, and that God would see us through this. She said ok, and we continued to hold each other for a long while. What a peaceful feeling. I did not want to scare her, but wanted her to know this was something to pray about. She fell asleep in my arms like she did when she was little.

My daughter Ella was 10, and a very sensitive girl. When she gets off the bus, she sings to herself all the way up the driveway. This is how I know she is home.

When I sat down to tell Ella, I simply told her that I was going to have a surgery. I told her there was something in my belly that needed to come out. She was okay with that and had just a couple of questions. Later, I learned that Ella really needed to know more than what I told her. Even though she was younger, she internalized a lot of the information, kept it in, and also found out some information from her friends and google, of course.

Later after my diagnosis, I remember Ella asking me, "Mommy, what stage is your cancer?" to which I answered and told her it was stage four. She was quiet, and then she asked, "What's after stage four, Mommy?' I told her Stage four wasn't good, but God is. She asked me to be honest with her about the details of my treatment. I promised I would. Each time I have a scan, I get texts from Ella from school asking me to tell her as soon as I know something. She has gone to each surgery and stayed in the hospital with me. My baby, who I thought was too young for this information, needs to know what is going on. It helps her to know.

My girls have each struggled in different ways during the past couple of years. I understand fully now how cancer does not just affect the patient, but the family, the caregivers, the children, the spouses. I hate it that my kids must even think about things such as this, but I know they will be stronger for it. They will be strong, amazing, women of God.

I hate the way that cancer has affected those around me. I will never forget the look of compassion that my little nephew Jack gives me when he visits me in the hospital. He brought me a little stuffed lion during my first hospital stay and before my second surgery. They are to help me be brave. The first time I lost my hair, Jack was sitting next me and asked me if I thought I might die. He then started crying. He was six years old at the time. I explained to him that God was going to help me fight and that I was strong and was going to try to stay on Earth for a long time and watch him turn into a big strong man. He hugged me and asked me to play on the playground with him. What a sweet precious boy. Children understand much more than we give them credit for.

I thank God for using this trial, this mountain, this cancer in our lives to grow us. I am still growing into the woman that God intended me to be. I feel His calling on my heart still. God will be Glorified through this. I hear his words, not audibly, but I hear them. He tells me, "Trust Me." Trust in Him. So I do.

Chapter 5

February 12, 2015 was the night before my first surgery. I had

to sit with my back reclined so that I could breathe. The fluid

from the swelling of the tumors in my abdomen was pressing up

on my diaphragm. The medical term for this is *ascites*. It means

that fluid was collecting in my abdominal cavity. The diaphragm

is the muscle that helps you to breathe. Basically, it felt as if I

was drowning in my own lungs. I had to talk quietly, and would

start coughing if I laughed or moved around too much. I was able

to stay comfortable if I was in the right position. On this night, I

wrote letters to my girls, went through pictures, tried to relax and

enjoy being home, and visited with family. My biggest fear, as a

mother, was not waking up from surgery.

February 13, 2015 is the date of my diagnosis. It was my surgery date. My doctor was expecting to find a tumor on my ovary, the one they saw in the CT scan. It was approximately 12cm. During the surgery, they would biopsy the tumor and determine what the rest of the surgery would entail. Many of my family members were there that day. As I was prepped for surgery I remember many of them in my room. We talked, joked, and some cried. I felt a peace over me. Many were praying for me, and I felt those prayers hitting me like a wave of calm. At that time, my nurse was also giving me some medicine to make me relax. I guess I told some pretty funny jokes for a minute and then I was out.

When I woke up, I was groggy. I have memories of certain things, but also other things I don't remember that were told to me. I do remember my mom at my side, telling me, "I love you. They got it all. They said it was on your colon. It's Colon Cancer. It was on your ovary too." I remember saying, "Well, I'm glad they got it all." I was glad she was there with me.

Later at some time I was told what this meant and what happened during my surgery. My doctor expected to open me up and remove a tumor from my ovary, test it, and either deal with ovarian cancer or just a benign tumor. Instead, when he opened me, he could see right away that the cancer originated in my colon. It had gone through the wall of the colon, invaded the ovary, and a large tumor was there also. I was open and he was not able to do my colon surgery. However, at the very same time, a colon team had just finished a surgery. They were available, called, and scrubbed in to do my surgery. Anyone who has ever tried to schedule a surgery knows what a miracle this is. A team there, ready, willing, called and going to do my surgery. You may say what a coincidence. I say there are no coincidences. That was God!

The colon team removed 12 inches of my colon and resected it. That means they connected the loose ends and I did not wake up with a colostomy bag. Then the original surgical team proceeded with their part of the surgery, which was a total hysterectomy. Instant menopause at age forty-three. I am not allowed to take any hormones to help with this because of the cancer and medicines I am on.

I was in the hospital for about a week and came home to heal. This surgery was major. I did feel so much better after the surgery, though. The pressure from the large tumor on my ovary and the one in my colon was relieved and the fluid was gone. I was told I would need to heal for about six to seven weeks and then would start chemo to ensure that any cancer cells floating around would be taken care of. I was told that since the cancer had left the original site, and spread to another organ, that this was Stage 4 colon cancer. As a nurse, I knew what this meant.

Many friends and family came to visit. Most were shocked of the news of what had happened and afraid for what was to come. I was also afraid, and went through many emotions. Night time was the hardest time for me. It was when I was alone with my thoughts. It was also then that I would hear the voice, or feel it rather.... "Trust Me." And so I did.

Chapter 6

Life did not stop. Time kept going. My girls still had school every day, and sports and extracurricular activities to get to. I did my best to keep 'normalcy' for them and in our household. I had lots of help from friends, family and people from our church. It was hard to give up control and accept help. This was something I had to surrender. I have never been one to accept a gift without giving one in return, however, during this time right after my diagnosis many people rallied and brought dinner for us. They helped me with the girls, with the house, and raised money for us to help us through this time.

It was difficult to say okay to the outpouring of financial blessings we received. However, it allowed me to take my mind off of the financial stress of not being able to work and added expenses of my cancer treatment. It also enabled me to do things for and with my girls that we would not otherwise be able to do.

I remember the first card I received in the mail after coming home. It contained a financial blessing, a hundred-dollar bill. I lost control of my emotions at that instant. It was the first time I had cried since the beginning of my diagnosis. It was good to cry and get some of my feelings out. Things happened so quickly that I never really had a chance to let things sink in. The money was so needed at the time, and the thought that someone would give to us in that way was just overwhelming. We were blessed by many people during this time. I will never be able to thank anyone enough for the help we received. Although money cannot heal cancer, it can relieve the additional stress that not being able to generate income can create. I had just graduated nursing school, and had planned to start working as an RN. Instead, I was a patient. A cancer patient. My husband and I were not prepared for this life changing and debilitating experience.

My friends, family and even people we didn't know were the hands and feet of Jesus during this time. I am ever grateful for the help we received. During this time, I felt the prayers of many. I was faced with one of my worst fears, that my girls would have to grow up without me. But I felt peace. Peace through the storm, through the trial, through this big mountain that was in my way. I have felt this peace throughout the past couple of years many times. Before each of my three surgeries, before and during a chemo treatment, I have felt the peace of God, through prayer. Through my prayer and through the prayers of others on my behalf.

It was also during this time that my friends and family got

together and started planning what is now known as our annual 'Have a Little Faith' Benefit concert. The first concert was in June of 2015, just four months after my first surgery and diagnosis. I agreed to my friends and family doing this on one condition. Every year this concert would continue. We would choose a recipient, someone newly diagnosed with late stage colon cancer, each year to bless. If I wasn't here to do this then they would continue with the concert every year. They agreed to this. This is a tradition that I plan to continue for many years to come. We are now preparing for our third concert. We are blessing a young woman who was recently diagnosed with Stage 4 colon cancer as well. She is thirty-six, a young wife and mother to two small children. Please pray for her. God knows her name.

Colon cancer is on the rise. It is not just for the elderly. Last year's concert recipient was thirty years old. Married and a father of two babies. He is doing well today and still needs prayer as well.

The concert that my friends and family gave me in June of 2015 was magical. It carried me through my liver resection, just ten days after the concert. It brought so many people together. I will never forget that special night and the love I felt. It carried me through the dark days that followed.

Concert performers gathered around me in prayer after a magical night of music and fellowship. June 6, 2015.

Chapter 7

After my surgery in February, the plan was for me to heal for five weeks and then to start chemotherapy to make sure there were no cancer cells remaining. In the meantime, I was healing and losing weight like never before. I lost twenty pounds on the operating table, and forty more in the weeks that followed after I had started Chemotherapy. I was looking very healthy and fit at this time, but feeling weak and like my body was betraying me. I felt like my body was dying, slowly.

During the month of March, before I would start chemotherapy in April, I met with my oncologist. He was a very nice man, with A LOT of information for us. The information was overwhelming. He explained how metastatic cancer works and what we could expect.

Metastasis is the medical term for cancer that spreads to a different part of the body from where it started. When this happens, doctors say the cancer has "metastasized." Other names for metastasis are "metastatic cancer" and "stage 4 cancer." Sometimes the term "advanced cancer" also describes metastatic disease, but this isn't always true. For instance, "locally advanced" cancer is not the same as metastatic cancer. It describes cancer that has spread to nearby tissues or lymph nodes but not throughout the body. (Cancer.net)

He went on to explain the chemotherapy and how it works. He explained side effects, and what to expect. He went further to tell me that my life expectancy would be 6 months without treatment and possibly around 36 months with treatment. *Wait. What? What did he just say? That is not going to work for me. Ella is 10. Olivia is 14. Three years. Three years?* The rest of what the oncologist was talking about did not make it into my ear. Rambling. *Three years.* These words kept playing in my mind, and sometimes still do, but very rarely now. I only discussed this with a couple of people. But it played through my mind a lot in the beginning. *Six months to three years.* Before we left the oncologist's office that day, I told my doctor that I appreciated him being honest with me, but that was simply not going to be the case with me. I told him I serve a Greater Physician, the Ultimate Healer, my Savior Jesus Christ. My oncologist agreed with me, and told me that he believed that also. That is how I knew this was the doctor I should stay with. So we scheduled for my port to be placed and for a body scan. Chemotherapy would start soon after my port was placed.

Not long after, I received a phone call about the scan results. I was sitting at lunch with Olivia and Ella as my nurse told me that the scan showed that the cancer had now spread to my liver. I had to keep that news to myself for a little while. *My heart dropped.* The girls and I enjoyed our day. Later that afternoon I shared the news with family and then later that evening in a Facebook post. God has put it on my heart to share my story. Facebook is one way that I have been able to put my feelings into words. God has now called me to share this further, thus the reason for this book. I never thought of myself as a writer. But it is my duty to share this story. His story. One of healing, hope, and the power of Jesus Christ. The following excerpt is my Facebook post from March 28, 2015.

March 28, 2015

I am struggling to find words to post, as the scan was not clear as we had hoped and prayed for. Although I feel weak, and am a little discouraged, I will stand firmly in my belief that God knows my name. He knows my pain and He knows my needs.

He will heal me completely, as is in His will. A friend sent this to

me today, and it brings me peace to know it is okay that I don't

understand why or how this could happen to me, that I am

afraid.....but to continue to lean on Him and trust in His amazing

love and healing. Proverbs 3:5-6 Trust in the Lord with ALL your

heart and lean not on your own understanding. In ALL your

ways acknowledge HIM and He WILL direct your path. Thank

you all for continued love, support and prayers.

Many people replied to this post and more people started

praying. Again, I felt these prayers. It helped me make it

through the night and through the days that followed.

Chapter 8

But fear consumed my mind yet again. The thought of the cancer in my liver terrified me. I feel like the next couple of weeks were spent in a daze. My mind was like a superhighway of thoughts. One minute I would be assuring my girls that I was strong and would be okay, and the next minute I was staring into space wondering how much more time I had with them. It was hard to keep my mind in the place it needed to be to continue this fight.

I believe that the mind has control over the body. I had to keep my mind strong, so that my body could fight. I did this by reaching out to my spiritual mentors and family for reassurance. I wanted to do all that I could to survive this cancer. But it felt like my life that had just been spared was again hanging from a cliff. All of reality was telling me that this cancer was going to kill me, sooner than later. Statistics said that I had an 11% chance to be alive in five years. My doctor said that the cancer was incurable. That he had seen many people do well, but the average expectancy was six months to three years. Again, those words. I tried to listen only for God's voice, but I was in a daze.

Now, as I am writing, it has been 26 months since my diagnosis. I do not live according to reality. I live according to faith. This is not to say that fear and doubt do not sometimes occupy my mind, but I will not let those thoughts remain there. God is my Healer. He is the Great Physician. As a disciple of Christ, we have power through the Holy Spirit. I will not rely on facts and figures, nor statistics. I will rely on my Heavenly Father, who knows exactly what I need, and when I need it.

2 Corinthians 5:7 For we live by faith, not by sight.

Chapter 9

The weeks that followed were still frightening for me. No matter what I was doing, the thought was always in the back of my mind. This might be my last softball season, birthday, Halloween, Christmas. I tried to make each day special. I made sure that the girls had normalcy, as much as possible, that they were able to participate in their activities. I tried to keep my mind focused on healing. At times I felt strong, but always in the back of my mind these thoughts were on the prowl. They were like a growling tiger that I couldn't see.

I was strong for my girls, because that's what moms do. I was strong during the daytime. Night time was harder. Sometimes it felt like reality was whispering in my ear, *"You can't do this. Why do you think you can survive these statistics? Three years if you're lucky."* Every ache or pain had me convinced that the cancer was invading another part of my body. While I tried to keep my thoughts and heart focused on God's promises, my eyes and ears were being taunted with man's words. I shared my thoughts with my closest of friends and family. They reminded me of God's promises. They reminded me how strong I am. They encouraged me when I was down. I relied on those that God had placed around me for the strength that I couldn't find.

God had placed some amazing and strong people around me. I didn't see how well he had orchestrated my life until I felt like it was falling apart. Sometimes it takes falling into the pit to open the eyes of our heart. I am no one special, I am not perfect, I am far from it. But here God was, by my side. Answering prayers. Assuring me to Trust Him. And so I did.

Chapter 10

Chemo began. The first day I went in for treatment, I didn't know what to expect. I wondered if I would be able to feel the poison that was going to be injected into my body. The chemo medicines are made to target the cancer cells. Although the chemo is given to kill the cancer cells, it damages other normal cells as well. Would I feel the medicine dripping into my body? Would it burn? Each drug has its own set of side effects. Some were gradual and some were immediate. I was warned of them prior to starting my chemo, but didn't fully understand until I felt them myself.

I was given three different drugs through my port, which is a tube that goes into my chest, just under my right clavicle, and into an artery that carries the blood from the heart throughout the body.

The port just looks like a bump under my skin, like a grape or something of that size. It is wonderful and serves its purpose. I have been asked if the port hurts or is uncomfortable. It's really just like part of my body now. It can get sore if it is bumped, but really it is not a hindrance to me. I am thankful that instead of getting an IV and damage to my smaller veins and arteries in my arms, that the port is able to be used to administer my meds. To answer the question about what the chemo feels like when it is pumped into the body, I could not actually feel the medicine going in, to my relief. However, depending on the type of chemo, some effects would be felt right away and others would be gradual or felt later. In general, I would be very tired during and after a chemo treatment. This kind of tired is not the kind of tired I have ever felt before. This was a debilitating tired. I slept for long periods in the days right after a treatment, and still required more sleep even weeks later.

For the first ten months or so, I was on a chemo medicine that had to be given in a pump. I would wear the pump home the day of treatment, and it would administer the chemo over the next three days. I remember the first time I received this medicine it made my body feel very heavy. This was a gradual effect, so that each time I received a treatment, every two weeks, the effect would increase. I also remember having pain in my legs, like I had run a marathon, but of course I hadn't.

I was trying to fix my hair one morning the day after a treatment, but my arms were so heavy I could barely brush my teeth. Other side effects I experienced in the first year of treatments were a burning rash on my face and neck, like a sunburn from the inside out. This really bothered me, as it was very noticeable and made me look like I had very bad acne or a skin infection of some kind. I got used to this side effect, and it stopped when that medicine was discontinued.

The drug that I call 'the devil' gave me my worst side effects. I could not be near cold. Walking through the grocery store next to the freezers was painful. Opening my own refrigerator was impossible. I couldn't touch a cold can or box from the freezer, and ice felt like broken glass on my fingertips. Drinking anything above room temperature was not possible, as it felt like I was swallowing glass shards. I am not on this medicine currently and I hope that I don't have to be on it again. However, I do have to say that I sometimes feel like a superwoman with superhuman strength and endurance to have made it through those side effects, not to even mention the pain from surgery or the cancer.

I know that this strength came from Jesus. I know that He carried me through this time. When I look back at all that I have endured over the past two years, the only thing I have to say is, 'That is God'. My life has been spared several times. I don't know why.

But I do know that my purpose now is to share this story. For as long as He will let me, I will glorify His name. God has put it on my heart to tell the story of His Love and Healing to anyone who will listen. And so I will.

Chapter 11

Two of my wonderful friends accompanied me to my first chemo treatment. I call them my 'Him and my Hur' in reference to Exodus 17:12 in the Bible. I could feel that they were also afraid of the chemo medicines. These friends, my sister and brother, my parents and extended family and friends were what carried me through these days. My Him and my Hur prayed over every bag of medicine that was pumped into my body. They held my hands, prayed over me, sang to me, cheered for me, read to me, and cried with me. I never went to chemo alone. We started calling these treatments 'chemo parties', joking that we were so crazy that the nurses were going to kick us out. I would say, "What are they going to do, fire me?" There were times when we were quiet though, and times when my friends and family would pray over and talk with other patients being treated. We got to know several of them well. We also got to know and love the nurses who cared for me and so many others in the infusion room. I am grateful for their care and for the care given to me by my wonderful Doctor and Nurse Practioner.

There was one day when my Dad brought Chic-fil-A in for us and for all the nurses and other patients. I quickly became very popular in the infusion room. I cherish the time that my family and friends sacrificed to be with me in those hours. Some of the best conversations I have ever had were while I was sitting in a chemo chair. If you haven't taken the time to sit down with a parent or friend lately, I suggest you do so. The time I spent in the chemo chair has led to many heartfelt discussions and shared time with many friends and loved ones. Thank you to so many who held up my hands when I couldn't do it for myself, and who sat with me through these times.

Exodus 17:12 When Moses' hands grew tired, they took a stone and put it under him and he sat on it. Aaron and Hur held his hands up--one on one side, one on the other--so that his hands remained steady till sunset.

Chapter 12

The chemo treatments and side effects from the medicines left my body feeling very fatigued. More than just fatigued, I can't think of a word for it. Heavy, sore, old, poisoned. There were days when I would get up with the girls before school and then go back to sleep the minute they got on the bus. I would sometimes sleep all day, waking up to Ella singing while she came up the driveway. Other days I might have a visitor for lunch or go out and do some running myself. As long as I was able to recharge, I was able to function. I required more sleep than a toddler. Sleep was my favorite thing to do.

My girls are very busy, so I would try to keep up with their activities. I never missed a performance or a game unless I was in the hospital after a surgery. I hate missing their activities.

When I was in the hospital and couldn't be there, friends and family would send me pictures and updates of Ella's softball and volleyball games. I love to watch her play. I remember watching Ella at practice one afternoon early in the season. The wind was so cold, and I was on the chemo that made me sensitive to the cold. I sat with two sweatshirts, three blankets, gloves and a hat while other parents sat in jeans and a sweatshirt. There was no way I was going to miss watching my baby play ball. I once had to miss Olivia singing the National Anthem for a sold-out crowd at a Butler Men's basketball game. I was in the hospital during this game for my second surgery and hated to miss this special night. I was listening to her in the hospital, though. Oh, it was beautiful. Thank goodness for technology!

Chapter 13

I started doing a lot of research about what was happening in my body. At first, the information scared me so much that I couldn't look at it. As a nurse, I know a little bit about cancer and what I was dealing with, but the more informed I was, the more power I felt over things. I sought a second opinion.

The doctor I met with was genuine and open. He agreed with what my doctor had told me, that this cancer is not curable, that I may have to do chemo for life, which would likely be shortened by Colon Cancer. However, he was able to offer a surgery to remove the cancer from my liver. Doing this would give me a better chance to live longer. It wouldn't guarantee that I would live longer or that the cancer wouldn't come back, but it was my best chance for survival. I had two spots on my liver, one being very close to a major artery. This surgery would be intense. I was told the recovery from this surgery could take up to 12 months. It was hard to believe that, until after I had the surgery.

I went in on June 16 of 2016. Family and friends supported me by wearing the Mustard Seed shirts that my sister had made for me. Many were praying. Many people, some that I didn't even know. I felt these prayers again, like a wave of peace. A peace that I couldn't understand, because I was fearful of this procedure and of the cancer. Friends and loved ones gathered at my home the night before. I remember being prayed over, and feeling just total peace. A calm like no other.

Phillipians 4:7 And the peace of God, which transcends all understanding, will guard your hearts and your minds in Christ Jesus.

When I awoke from my liver resection, I was in intense pain. I was groggy. I was thirsty. I remember being so thirsty and only being able to suck on a little green sponge on a stick. What is this, anyway? This was my post-surgical snack each time I had surgery. I wanted a big glass of water. A cup of ice. Something, please. Why did I have to suck on this little green sponge?! I think I was even mad at my sister who was serving me the spongy treat, because she wasn't giving it to me fast enough! She said I gave her a scary look. Oh, bless my sister Jenny and my sweet Mommy who did everything for me that I couldn't do for myself while I was healing in the hospital. The nurses were helpful, but they were not my sister. They were not my mommy. As old I as get, I don't think I'll ever stop wanting my mom when I don't feel good.

The reason for the little sponge, by the way, is to limit the amount of fluids entering into the stomach and intestines after surgery. It was a long time before I could have fluids of any kind and even longer before I could eat any kind of food. You would think that would make me lose weight, but I actually gained a lot of weight during and after this operation. So much for those cute jeans I bought after losing weight.

The day after my surgery, I was awake. I couldn't see myself, but I guess I was sort of a yellowish color. My amazing surgeon had removed 65% of my liver containing the cancer. The whole right lobe and gall bladder and part of my left lobe had been removed. I immediately went into liver failure. Although the doctors knew that this would happen, my family did not.

I was not really myself. My thoughts and dreams were odd. I really can't remember most of what I dreamed about, but I know my mind was playing tricks on me. This was because of the bilirubin that was building up in my body. I was being watched closely by doctors and nurses and my family was assured that this was normal and that I was doing well. The pain. Was. Intense.

At one point, I remember looking at my cell phone. I knew that I had received texts from my girls and from others. I could see that I had new messages, but I could not figure out how to press the buttons and get my phone to do what I wanted it to do. I also remember looking at my phone and wondering what all of the letters meant. I asked my mom, "Mom, can I read?" I thought that I could, but I couldn't make sense of any letters or words. I lay there wondering if I could read or not, and hoped that I could.

Oh, the pain. Such pain. It is a good thing that our bodies do not let us remember exactly what the pain feels like. I can't describe it, other than by saying, I thought the pain alone was going to kill me. I thought if I made it out of this hospital that it would be a miracle. I did make it out of the hospital, ten days after my surgery I was released to go home. I could read again, and I wasn't yellow anymore.

Coming home felt wonderful. My girls and my sweet nieces and nephew decorated my living room with posters and balloons and were there to greet me. The walk from the van to the front door was so difficult. Remembering it now as I write, I am amazed at the way our bodies are designed. God has made our bodies with the amazing ability to heal, and not only that, but has left us the power to heal ourselves. Again, I thought the pain alone was going to kill me. But it did not.

My friends and family again had to help me to function. Olivia and Ella helped me walk to the bathroom and back. It exhausted me. After a couple of days at home I wanted to take a shower. I had to ask my daughter Olivia for help getting undressed, showered, dried and dressed again. She took such good care of me. I told her I was so sorry she had to help me with these things and I never thought I would be in this position where she would have to take care of me instead of me taking care of her. She said, "Mom, I would do this every day. I love you and don't worry about it." She was fifteen at the time. I was in such pain and the whole process exhausted me. Then there was sleep. Lots of sleep.

A couple of weeks later when I was feeling stronger, Olivia and Ella took me on a walk through my neighborhood. We walked down the road and back. It was a beautiful summer evening and a memory I will always treasure. Both of them by my side, walking so slowly, just talking. Stopping for me to catch my breath often.

Although it seemed like it took forever to heal from that surgery, I was feeling stronger and stronger week by week. I think at about six months I was able to lay on my side. It is still not comfortable, but I'm a side sleeper and was excited to be able to lay on my side again. I'm glad to say that my liver is still free of cancer.

The liver, by the way, is the only organ in our body that can regenerate! I liked to joke and say that God did that because He knew I'd need a new liver. Lol. My doctor didn't think that was very funny, but I did. I'm usually the one to laugh at most of my jokes actually. That's what my kids tell me. Laughter has been a great way to deal with things also. When all else fails, tell a silly joke and laugh.

Ecclesiastes 3:4 a time to weep and a time to laugh, a time to mourn and a time to dance

Chapter 14

Looking back on the months right after my initial diagnoses, I can see now the plans that God had for my life. The events that have occurred, as I'm looking back, were intricately planned.

Something that Ella and I like to say is that 'Good things can come from bad things.' I will say that many good things have come because of this bad thing, this cancer, my trial, my mountain. God has used this to mold me into the woman He created me to be. I see now His plans for me. I don't know what they are still, but I am learning to listen for His voice in my decisions. I am learning to give up the control that I thought I had and to give Him power over my life. I have learned that we are in control of nothing. He is in control of all things.

I will never forget Ella using that quote 'good things come from bad things' when she was enjoying some wonderful dinners that were delivered to us after my surgeries. We were blessed by many people bringing meals and joy into our home during that time.

Another great thing that has come from this mountain are the mended relationships. A friend I hadn't talked to in years called me not long after my diagnosis. "What is it that I'm mad at you about anyway?" she said. She told me she was a bad friend because it took me getting cancer for her to call me. She is a wonderful long-time friend and I am so thankful for her.

I have been able to spend quiet time with my brother, my dad, and several other family members. As they sat with me through treatments or drove me to and from treatment centers, the moments we spent talking are priceless. I am thankful for the time that I have been able to spend with so many who are special to me.

I am also thankful for the time I have been able to spend with my oldest daughter, Jordan and her husband. Two of the most genuine people that I know. I am so thankful for the times they sat with me while I was healing from a surgery or a treatment. They always have me laughing. They have also given me another reason to fight, as I will be a Grandma this summer! I cannot wait to love on that baby boy and to sing to him.

God has allowed me to enjoy so much during the past couple of years even through the struggles and pain. I know I have much more to do here, and so much to live for. I am excited for the future and look forward to living. There is so much to live for.

Life is wonderful, even with all of its trials. Each day is a gift. I am learning to 'live in the moment' as my friend Erika used to say.

Jeremiah 29:11 For I know the plans I have for you,"

declares the LORD, "plans to prosper you and not to

harm you, plans to give you hope and a future.

Chapter 15

As I got stronger after my liver resection, I began working some short hours for a home health company as an RN. I was thankful to use my RN license and to be doing something important. I had felt like I was doing a lot of nothing, although I was able to travel with Ella's softball team and to keep up with my kids.

I was still getting chemo treatments every two weeks and was feeling better. In November of 2016, I had a scan that showed *No Evidence of Cancer!*

I was so happy but could hardly believe it. As I told friends and family of the news, many of them cried happy tears. Everyone took this to mean the cancer was gone. Gone. It was gone, but I could still hear the growling in the background. As much as I wanted to celebrate this amazing news, I was still fearful to claim it. Every pain or ache put fear in me that the cancer was back. I so wanted to believe that it was gone, but I felt it would be back.

That is when I confronted myself with this thought. If God had healed me, why would He allow this to come back. If I truly believed that He had the power to heal, then why was I doubting the fact that the cancer could be gone? It was brought to my attention that I was limiting God. I would believe that He could heal me but then would wonder if He really could.

Well, I struggled with this thought and I do believe it did hinder my healing. As I said before, the mind controls the body. And God controls it all. So, to truly expect healing, I had to *believe* that this could happen. Not believe it some of the time, or believe it half way, but truly believe it!

Well, the cancer did in fact come back. It was early in 2016 that I had another scan, showing the cancer had spread into my peritoneal lining and also into my pelvis. It had now been in my colon, my ovaries, my liver, and now my peritoneal lining and in my pelvis. I took this news very hard. The cancer was spreading even while I was on maintenance chemo. This cancer just wasn't going to stop! Fear and even despair came over me.

This news knocked me to the floor. It took me a couple of weeks to pull myself up. I wasn't literally on the floor for two weeks, but I wanted to be. Just lying flat on the floor. I finally had to claim healing again. God has done this before. Why would He forsake me now? I listened for His voice, but it was hard to hear.

My biggest fear was that I wouldn't make it to Christmas of this year. *Oh, Father please let me make it through Christmas. Please don't take me from my girls.* The doctor I was seeing at the time suggested we start a new chemo cocktail, for as long as it would work. I knew God had better plans for me. I prayed. And listened. And prayed. And was still.

I was watching TV late at night when the commercial for a large cancer center in Illinois came on. I had seen this commercial before, several times, but this time I saw it differently.

I called and scheduled an initial appointment. I would have to travel four hours from home for each appointment. I felt a new hope in this place, although I was still fearful. My first appointment with them was in June of 2016. During my first appointment with them, I talked with a surgeon about a procedure I had been reading about. I felt it was my only hope for longevity, and was seeking this treatment. The procedure was Cytoreductive surgery and HIPEC. The surgeon told me it was the mother of all surgeries.

I said I had already heard that about my liver resection. He said, yes, this is the mother to that. *Ohhhh* I was nervous but still pushed for this surgery. I was advised to start a strong chemotherapy regimen before this surgeon would agree to operate on me. The surgeon wanted to know that the cancer would respond to the chemotherapy medicines that would be used during the surgery and after. Otherwise, the surgery would just take away my quality of life and not give a benefit.

Although I was given hope at this new place, I was also given more information. The surgeon was very honest with us and said this surgery would extend life, but would not cure the cancer. I thought, "He doesn't know what God can do". I still believe this. Watch me prove it.

So, we began the new treatment in hopes that I would qualify for surgery. We made each trip to Illinois as fun as we could. Every three weeks, someone would go with me on this mini-vacation of sorts. The hospital was close to a beautiful lake, where we would play on the beach and throw rocks. The hotels were nice and I looked forward to the hot tub when it was working.

I was advised not to sit in a hot tub, but I do anyway. Too many germs. I continue to do the things I enjoy. I just pray for God's protection if I decide to get into a germ infested hot tub or a room full of sneezing and coughing kids. Better to enjoy life than just sit in a box and try not to get sick. I am not advising anyone who is currently on chemotherapy meds to do this, I just know what works for me. I am very careful about germs and hand washing, and try to stay away from sick people. I did play in the dirt as a child, so I think in general my immunity is pretty strong.

The chemo causes low immunity. My white blood cells and platelets are usually low even right before a treatment. This is why they advise to be careful about germs. Don't be around sick people, don't eat raw vegetables and fruits, don't do this, don't do that. I am careful, but who doesn't want to sit in a hot tub every once in a while? I decided to make the best choices that I could to keep myself safe, but to also still enjoy the little things.

Chapter 16

The chemo cocktail that I started in Illinois consisted of three drugs, different than the ones before. No more pump. That drug was now given to me in a pill. I would take that medicine, 4 huge pills, in the morning and before bedtime for two weeks. I would take one week off and then start that cycle again. I am still currently taking that drug.

The worst part of this chemo regimen was a drug that caused hair loss and GI Upset. *GI Upset.* That is a very nice term for what happened inside my stomach and intestines. This made a normal day difficult but travel almost impossible. However, I was able to enjoy a wonderful trip with one of my best friends and my sister to Las Vegas. This gave the saying 'What happens in Vegas, stays in Vegas' a whole new meaning, as I visited every restroom along the Vegas strip! We were there the first month that I started on this medicine, and the 'GI upset' had never been so bad. I didn't let this spoil our fun. Las Vegas was still amazing. We had a wonderful trip and even got to see one of our favorite performers, Celine Dion. I was, by the way, able to sit through her entire concert with having to make a trip to the restroom. Thank you, Sweet Jesus.

Chapter **17**

Hair loss. My hair had thinned in the first year of treatment, but this new medicine was known for hair loss.

This past July, I was in Zion with my daughters for treatment. Jordan, Olivia, Ella and I decided to make a fun vacation out of this couple of days we had to be in Illinois.

I loved spending this time with Jordan and the girls. Jordan is married to a wonderful man that we all adore. She is in dental school, so time with her is precious. We laughed so hard, had wonderful talks, listened to music and sang our hearts out on the way there. This was my favorite trip to Zion. We ate our lunch at the lake on the beach and rode a train into Chicago for some fun.

Oh, we also went to the hospital and got my chemo infusion. I slept through it and the girls sat by my side.

Chicago with the girls was wonderful. We got there later in the afternoon, but were still able to enjoy the sites and took lots of pictures.

We rode a boat taxi to the Navy Pier. This is when Olivia noticed my hair falling out, in little wisps. Blowing into the wind, into her face! We were laughing. I lost my whole head of hair during the three days that we were there. Little by little, it fell out. Some people shave their head as soon as the hair starts to fall out. I said I was going to hold onto every last bit. I came home with one wisp of hair on top of my head.

It wasn't a terrible experience. If I would have lost all of my hair at home I think it would be different. We were having a blast. Laughing, enjoying each other. I wasn't thrilled that my hair was falling out, but there were certainly worse things that could happen. 'No hair, don't care' was our motto.

My oldest daughter and her sweet mommy, also my friend, had arranged for me to visit with a hairdresser, a friend of theirs, after we got home. She shaved my remaining wisps of hair off and took me for a wig fitting. She treated me to a beautiful wig and would not accept payment. I was so blessed and am thankful for my wig as my hair has fallen out completely twice. I am used to being without my hair noq, and I actually like the short pixie cut that I am growing. But sometimes a girl likes to have some pretty hair. It looks just like mine did before I was diagnosed. I am so grateful for this gift of new hair.

The weirdest thing about losing my hair were the looks that I got from people when I was in public. These people looked at me like I had cancer! Yes, I had been walking around feeling miserable, going through cancer treatments, had two major surgeries, but when I lost my hair then people thought I actually had cancer. It's okay, I thought the same thing before my diagnosis. Cancer does not look the same on everyone.

I've also learned that hair is over-rated. I love not having to spend time drying or straightening my hair. I have gotten used to the way I look. Cancer and treatments have changed the way I look and the way I feel. I have learned to love the person that I am regardless of how I look. I am learning to see myself as beautiful, even with my flaws. I wish I had known this long ago. I spent a lot of time looking pretty and feeling ugly. Why do we do this to ourselves? I wish people could see themselves the way the world sees them, or better yet, the way God sees them.

I still struggle with self-image, as many of us do. This happens especially when trying on clothes or getting ready to go somewhere, but then I think how thankful I am to be in this body. Thank you, God. Thank you for letting me stay in this body, with all its flaws. I have much more to do here. Thank you, Sweet Jesus. I am so blessed.

Photo Album

Surrounded by best friends, love, prayers and laughter for a chemo treatment.

Dressed for my first position as an RN. I worked part time as a home health nurse when I was well enough. This was three months after my liver resection.

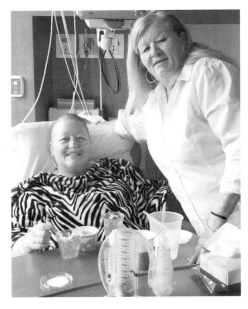

My sweet Mommy was by my side after every surgery. She did everything for me that I couldn't do for myself.

Me and mom on the beach at Lake Michigan. This spot was ten minutes from the hospital I went to in Illinois. Everyone that came to Illinois with me visiting this spot. Lots of rock throwing happened here. Many great memories.

My baby brother and little sister.

My first best friends.

Denise and Katie, 'my Him and my Hur' bringing some Hawaiian sunshine into the infusion room. These two were always dressing up, singing, praying and making me and others laugh.

At home not long after my liver resection. My skin was a nice tint of orangish-yellow. I am snuggling with my little lion that Jack gave me to help me stay brave.

Thank you, Jack!
You are my best boy ever!

I always feel safe when my Dad is with me. I'm so very thankful for the many heartfelt talks we were able to have when he was at treatment with me. My favorite drives to Illinois were with my Dad. I treasure the time we spend together.

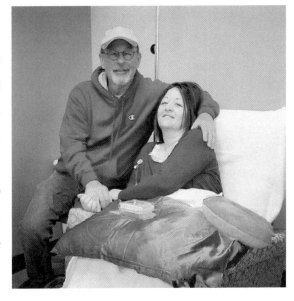

Summer of 2015. This was a great family trip even though I felt very sick. This picture is in black and white, but even in color my skin was grey.

Sis and Brother with me at the cancer center in Illinois. This was a

tough day for all of us. Mom was there also, but was very sick. She ended up in the hospital as well that day. Praise God, as we brought her home with us the next week.

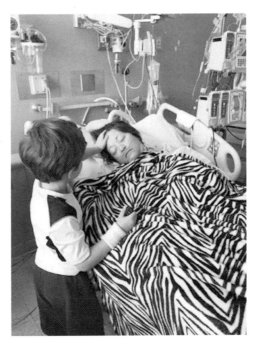

Sweet Jack.
My best boy ever.

In Vegas with my Nenny and my Heather. Didn't let that chemo ruin our fun.

Stopped at every bathroom on the Vegas strip though!

A dear friend and spiritual mentor reading from the Bible at one of my treatments.

My mommy and her sisters. All strong. All beautiful and amazing.

'Eagles When they Fly'

Two-time breast cancer survivor, Aunt Nancy, lower right.

Fun in Chicago with my girls.

Every time the wind blew, I lost a

little bit more hair.

We had the best time and laughed

all weekend!

"No hair, Don't care!"

My Sissy.

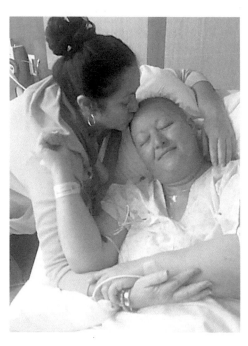

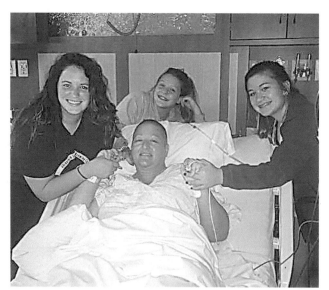

My amazing girls.

My heart.

'Squirrelapalooza' 2016. Two months after my HIPEC surgery.
Dad and Jeanne and the crew.

Fall of 2016. Ella's volleyball tournament. Not long after my HIPEC surgery. Only a hospital bed can keep me from watching this girl play!

Baby Therapy. Baby Brooklyn kept me company several times after a treatment. That along with Aunt Joyce's noodles was good medicine!

My 'sister cousin' Jessi and Aunt Joyce loving on me after HIPEC surgery in September of 2016.

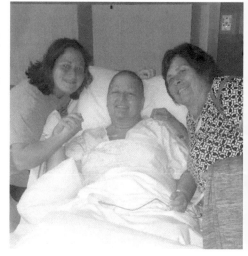

Chapter 18

After several trips to Zion, Illinois, it was time to meet with my surgeon again to see if I qualified for the HIPEC surgery. This surgery would not 'cure' the cancer, but it would add time to my life. The doctor said it would be like setting the clock back to zero.

He talked about quality of life vs. length of life. It was quite a decision to make. I felt like I was flipping a coin and neither side was the winner. I tried to listen for God's voice. I was reminded that this is what we came here for. Hope. Choices. Another option. I believed strongly that getting the cancer out of my body was the best chance at survival. I knew this surgery would be difficult, and it was very risky. I was almost certain it was what I wanted to do. My surgeon told me that this surgery may add a year or two to my life. A year or two is better than none, but as I have said

before, I do not rely on man's word. I rely on God's Word. Man's

word doesn't work for me. It doesn't work for my girls. I know

that God has the ability to heal, and I will proclaim this over and

over. Even when my mind doesn't believe it, I will still proclaim it

with my mouth. God is Bigger. He is able. He is Healer. He is King.

As I am typing this now I feel His presence. The thunder is rolling

outside, and I feel like these are His words, not mine. ***Trust.***

Believe. Trust Me. I will not forsake you.

I decided to go forward with the surgery.

September 21, 2016 was the date scheduled for surgery. It would

be a long procedure. My family was told it could be five to twelve

hours. Mom and Dad and sweet stepmom Jeanne, my sister and

brother, and many others joined me in Zion. I had to prep for surgery so we were there for the three days prior to surgery as well. I was nervous and hoping I was making the right decision, and they were all nervous as well. We were still able to enjoy each other and to laugh. Oh, the laughter. There was never a dull moment with all of us. My nurses were also entertained by my family. It was so wonderful to have them there.

The morning of my surgery we gathered and waited. Many of my family were wearing their Mustard Seed shirts. They gathered around me and prayed over me before I was rolled back to prepare for surgery. I asked my surgeon one last time, "Do you think this surgery is a good idea?". He replied, "If I didn't think so, then I wouldn't be preparing you for surgery." I smiled and then drifted off. Peaceful sleep.

I woke from surgery to the sound of my family laughing again. Oh, sweet Jesus, that wonderful sound! I was in my hospital room and they were playing cards. I remember Ella laughing at Papaw and then when she saw I was awake she came over and gave me a giant hug. *Thank you Jesus that I woke up!* I was groggy, but I was awake, and of course thirsty. No water, only the green sponge. That green sponge again!

I was very tired so I went back to sleep to the sound of my family laughing and talking quietly. I loved that sound, it was wonderful to listen to as I drifted off again.

My surgeon was very happy with how things went. He said the surgery was successful. I was to get up and walk the next day. I was surprised at how easily I was able to get up and walk slowly through the hallway. I was smiling and giving the 'thumbs up' sign to everyone I walked by. I was amazed that I wasn't really in much pain at all.

I later learned that I still had the epidural pain block. It was removed on the third day, and I felt the most intense pain I have ever felt in my life. Getting out of my bed was incredibly difficult. I can't explain the pain other than to say I thought it was going to kill me. I thought something was wrong. The nurses kept telling me this was normal for the surgery I just had. I was thinking they certainly would not call this pain 'normal' if they could feel it. They would call it something else, I don't know what, but not 'normal'.

Many were with me in the hospital, but my mom never left my side. She kept the nurses in line and made sure they were taking good care of me. She did everything for me that I couldn't do, which was everything. I was able to walk up and down the hallway, but with great difficulty. The pain was great. Each day I walked a little further. I wondered if this surgery was such a good idea after all. *God, please let me go home to my girls.* I just wanted to go home. *Lord, please take this pain away.* The pain medication did not help. Only sleep helped. When I fell asleep, I couldn't feel the pain. *Jesus, am I going to make it home?*

I improved enough to be discharged by the hospital, although I thought they were crazy for letting me leave, as I was bleeding, leaking, hurting, and still thinking this surgery was going to kill me. When my mom and I left the hospital, we had to stay in a hotel nearby before we drove the four hours home. My surgeon didn't want me to leave the state yet, but wanted to release me from the hospital to test the waters. He wanted me close enough to go the ER if needed.

I left the hospital with a catheter and some drains coming from my belly to help with the swelling. It was hard to walk, to move, to lay down, to sit. I could not get comfortable no matter what I did.

Mom and I watched movies all night in the hotel. I was able to sleep a bit, but not well. I took my pain pills right on schedule, I couldn't wait to take the next one, and when I did, the pain didn't stop, but it was less.

We left for Indiana the next day. I got to go home! I slept most of the way home. I don't remember much of the first couple of days at home, only that I was so glad to be there.

I had a hospital bed in my living room and nurses who would come and check on me at home. After a few weeks, I started healing quickly. I was amazed at the energy that I had. I was able to walk to the end of the driveway and back, even around my neighborhood, in just a month. Healing was happening. God is Good. I was getting stronger.

Each month that passed it seemed that I was able to do more. I would get frustrated though, with something that I couldn't do. I still can't move quickly. After seven months, I have gained strength, but things like running or jumping just aren't possible, as it causes pain in my abdomen. I have to be careful with lifting, as I'm still at risk for a hernia and had a couple of water pockets that formed where tissue was taken out during my surgery. It hurts to lay on my stomach, so I don't. But even a nudge in the belly can cause great pain. I know that I am still healing and I try to be patient with myself, but it is frustrating at times. I want to do more than I am capable of right now, but I know I am getting stronger.

I am amazed, though, at what I CAN do. I can keep up with my girls. I can run them to their events and attend functions. I can play basketball with my nephew in the driveway. He's too fast for me, and he's a ball hog, but he lets me get a few shots in here and there. I'm able to do many things, and am getting stronger. I still tire easily. This is partly from the chemo I am currently taking, but also from the HIPEC surgery. I was told it would take a good year before I felt like myself. I found this to be true with my liver resection as well. It is amazing the way that God designed our bodies. That we can heal from such an ordeal. The human body amazes me. I am so thankful He designed us in this way!

Psalms 147:3 He heals the brokenhearted and binds up their wounds.

Chapter 19

This past year, we celebrated such a wonderful Christmas. We enjoyed the New Year and the excitement it brings. Our 'Marchabration' came and went. This is what we call the month of March, since we celebrate so many birthdays that month. Myself and my girls are born in March, as well as my sister, my cousin, and several others. It's just a big month of celebrating.

I remember when I was first diagnosed. Every holiday brought such anxiety and fear. Although I was still able to enjoy the holidays, and made sure that the girls did as well, the fear was at the back of my mind. It was that tiger growling. Would this be my last Christmas? Will I see these ornaments again? As I packed away the Christmas ornaments the first year, I enjoyed each one and the memories that came with them. I tried to make sure birthdays and holidays were special. I have always done this, but it took on a new meaning after my diagnosis. Would this be my last one? *Oh Lord, please don't take me from my girls.* Would I be here next Christmas? For the next birthday? For the next benefit concert? *Please let me see my girls graduate.* These things would fill my mind, but I was still able to enjoy the time.

This Christmas was different. I was able to enjoy the season more. I was able to enjoy the TIME more. This Marchabration, I found myself thinking about how we would celebrate next year. As I am planning our benefit concert for this June, I am also coming up with ideas for next year. I am planning to be here. I am at peace with giving God control over this mountain, this cancer. He knows what is best for me, and for my girls. I am learning to trust Him more and more. I still like to think I have control over things, but

I am always reminded that I don't. I have learned, we really have control over nothing. But God has control over everything.

God continues to tell me to Trust Him. I am listening. He tells me that He will Heal me. **_Trust Me. I've got this._** I am believing. **_Trust Me. Fully._** And so I do.

Proverbs 3:5-6 Trust in the LORD with all your heart and lean not on your own understanding; in all your ways submit to him, and he will make your paths straight.

Chapter **20**

Fall 2016 came and went after my HIPEC surgery. The change of seasons always brings hope and an excitement for the season to come. I would say that fall is my favorite season. I love the changing of the leaves, the smell of a good bonfire, the crispness in the air and a comfortable turtleneck.

My hair finally started growing back, and by Halloween I was sporting a cute pixie style. People would stop me and tell me how they loved my hair cut. I would thank them and think to myself, 'This isn't a haircut, it's a hair-grow.' I told this to a couple of people and they didn't get it. I don't know why I found it so amusing. That is usually the way my jokes work, though. I think they are pretty funny but they're really pretty goofy. I was still amused. My hair ended up falling out again in the spring, but is growing back nicely again now.

I was feeling better and started back on chemotherapy about six weeks after my surgery. My incision was healing nicely, and I now had a pretty decorated stomach with my many surgery scars, my battle wounds.

I liked to tell my little nieces and nephews that a tiger bit me on the belly, or that a shark had tried to get me while I was swimming in the pool, but they were too smart. They remembered that I had surgery a couple of times. They still liked my stories though. It's amazing how those little brains work.

I remember when my nephew Jack came to see me at the hospital, how observant he was. He had questions about what the tubes did, why that machine was beeping, and what were the things hooked up to me. Not only did he take all of that in, but weeks later he drew a picture of me lying in my hospital bed with the tubes and the machine, and even the doctor. It was a very detailed picture. My favorite part of it was that he put a smile on my face. The little ones always make me smile. My nieces and nephews have brought me so much joy. They have been good medicine!

Soon after Halloween, we had our annual 'Squirrelapalooza'. This is when Dad and his wife Jeanne, and my sis and brother and all of our kids go to Nashville, Indiana and stay in a cabin together. This is a tradition that we started just a couple of years ago, but one that we will definitely continue. After my diagnosis, I really wanted to spend time with loved ones. Time and people became more precious. Living in the moment became necessary. We made some great memories in Nashville. I'm looking forward to it again this fall.

Chemo continued every three weeks. I would travel to Illinois for a two or three day stay. One of my treatments fell on the week right after Christmas. We decided to make the best of it and my daughter invited a friend to go with me and my mother-in-love, Sis. The girls had fun and got to swim all day while I was at the hospital getting treatment. Sis enjoyed reading a book by the pool and then we had a wonderful dinner.

Trips to Zion were usually nice. Even though I was going there for chemo, we always tried to put some joy into the trip as well. After being treated for several months at the Cancer Center, I started to lose my joyful feeling in being there. I had gotten to know several other patients and would sometimes see them. Two of my new friends I met there passed early this year. It became harder to be joyful and full of hope, as the trip was sometimes exhausting and expensive. I began to feel the urge to bring my treatment closer to home soon after this. I decided I would be still, and listen for God's voice in what to do. He had led me where I needed to be throughout my treatment, and I wanted to make sure this yearning to return home for treatment was from Him and not just me thinking it would be easier to be close to home.

Several times I had been looking through some paperwork, and would come across this doctor's name. I had talked to him early on in my care and had decided not to seek treatment from him, but his name kept popping up. A friend even said to me, "Oh you should see this doctor in Indy, he is the best."

I decided to make an appointment with him at the Simon Cancer

Center in Indianapolis and I'm so glad I did! I have been seeing an excellent and highly recommended doctor who is known and loved by many. I am happy to be in his care, and I know that God is using him to heal me. God's plan is not always clear, but I see how He is laying things out. His plan is unfolding before my eyes.

I am currently doing a maintenance dose of chemotherapy every three weeks. It is enough to keep the cancer at bay, but not too much that it makes me feel terrible. I am now starting to feel more comfortable with this whole cancer thing. I am learning that I can live with cancer. I know that this cancer is never going to stop trying to take over my flesh, so our goal is to stay ahead of the game. Reality and statistics tell me that this cancer will take my life, sooner than later. Again, I have stopped listening to 'reality', because in fact, the only thing that I know is real, is God! I have seen just how REAL He is! He has lifted me from the pit so many times in my life. Not only through the past couple of years with this cancer, but other times as well. He has lifted me from the pit when I didn't deserve to be lifted out. But He did it anyway. If you have felt the presence of God then you know what I mean. If not, then I pray that you will surrender to the experience. No matter what your mountain is, it is never too big for God.

I had hoped for a break from chemo at some point, but I now understand that taking a break from chemo would be like giving cancer a playground. I can do this. I can do chemo.

Philippians 4:13 I can do all things through Christ who strengthens me.

Some say chemo for life. I say chemo for now, and we'll see. God is still Bigger. He is still the God of miracles. The same today as He was when Jesus walked the earth. Although I am accepting that I need to continue chemo to keep cancer at bay, I am also counting on the day when I can say, "I am cancer free!' I believe God is going to do this. I have much more to do. He tells me to Trust Him. And so I do.

Chapter 21

May 12, 2017

This past week, I had a PET scan. I usually have these about every six months. This type of scan shows cancer spots as a bright light on the screen. A sugar is injected into the veins with radioactive material that shows up on the scan. The cancer cells pick up the sugar quickly, making them light up.

This is where people get the idea that cancer loves sugar. Well, it does. Every cell does. Every cell in our body depends on sugar to function. Some cells 'pick up' or grab the sugar molecules faster than others, though. Cancer cells do this. It makes sense to me that sugar feeds cancer, but we cannot simply go sugar free to beat cancer. A healthy diet and a regulated or normal blood sugar is a good idea, in my opinion, to fight cancer, along with many other tools.

When I went in for the results of my scan, I was not sure what to expect. In the past, I have gotten a phone call from the nurse or I have been able to look at my own scan and radiology report prior to talking with the doctor. This time, I was walking in with no clue what my scan showed. I have gotten used to waiting for results of scans and tests. I have learned to put them out of my mind, knowing that whatever the results were, they just were.

Sitting in that room waiting was different, though. My oncologist finally walked in with a smile on his face and said he was very happy with the scan. He said it was pretty good.

He went over the scan with me and proceeded to tell me of a spot that was found on my spine. *Another place in my body. Cancer has invaded another place.* We talked about the scan further and I asked him where this spot was. It was located at T8. He said this was right in the middle of my back, along the bra line. This made sense to me. I told him of the pain I had been having. The pain is in the middle of my body, not really the back, but from the front to the back. It usually comes on late at night and doesn't stop hurting until I fall asleep. Tylenol and pain medicine do nothing to help this pain. I had not talked much about it. I have pains here and there that I attribute to the many surgeries I have had. Dr Helft confirmed that this is the kind of pain that spot on my spine would cause. Ugh, this wasn't the good news I had hoped for. I started to worry for a bit. It took me a couple of hours to get used to this news. But this is one spot. One spot. I have had Colon cancer in my colon, my ovary, my liver, the lining of my organs in my abdomen, and in my pelvis. Those have all been removed. My organs have had a hot chemo bath. There is no cancer right now anywhere except for this one spot. Well, Praise God! It took me just a little while for this news to sink in. But these results are great!

This is how I deal with cancer now. One little spot. God is Bigger. I can do this. I **must** do this.

My doctor spoke with me about how we could treat this spot. We plan to do radiation, which will shrink the cancer and also give pain relief. I will meet with a radiation specialist next week. I have not yet had radiation. This is new. I have been told that radiation makes you tired. I don't think I can be more tired than I have been, maybe I'll get lucky and it will give me energy or something. I just know that after all I have endured up til now, I know this is doable. Some people say that God won't give you anything that you can't handle. This is not true and will not be found in the Bible.

Instead, my friends and I say that God will not give you anything that HE can't handle! I know He can handle this, so I'm ready to move forward.

Remember, God won't give you anything that

HE can't handle!

Chapter 22

I hope that this book has blessed you. It is my desire that some part of my writing may have moved you in a way that will help you or someone else. In the final chapters I would like to simply share some of my previous writings. The following is a small excerpt that I wrote one day after finding out about another young life lost to colon cancer.

I called it 'What Can I Do?' and posted it on Facebook on December 16, 2015.

I lost another friend to stage 4 colon cancer today. Although I did not know Danielle well, I knew her. I knew her struggles, I knew her pain, I knew her heart. I knew she was a mom who loved her children dearly. I have been struggling recently, knowing that my life was spared, for how long I do not know. But also feeling lost and still trying to survive. What do I do with the time God is giving me?

So I came up with these things, and am also asking that all of you do these things. Please help me by joining me in 'living in the moment' as my dear friend Erika Hamilton would say.. also a young beautiful life taken by colon cancer.

What can you do to help me and also to honor Erika, Danielle, and so many others who are taken too soon by cancer. This is what I, and all of you, can do:

1. Love each other. Flaws and all. Love each other and forgive each other. Be nice.

2. Love God. Accept the gift of atonement (sins washed away) that Jesus offers to you.

3. If you don't know how to do number 2, or would like to know more about how to do this, ask me.

4. Love yourself. Accept yourself. Forgive yourself.

5. Insist on cancer screenings. I was 43 when I was diagnosed with metastatic stage 4 colon cancer. Normal screenings do not start until age 50. Get a colonoscopy. If you feel like something is wrong, insist on screening.

6. Treat your body like it belongs to someone you love. Take good care of yourself. People are depending on you.

7. Smile at strangers. Talk to people. Ask someone if they need help. Make eye contact. Make people feel important. Say please and thank you. Say I'm sorry.

8. Tell your children you love them, no matter what. Tell them they cannot do anything to make you not love them. Tell them this even if they are grown up, but especially when they are little. Tell them that as much as you love them, God loves them even more. It's true.

9. Pray. Believe that your prayers will be answered. Praise God for the work He will do, and for the work He is doing. Wait. Pray more. Praise God more. Pray.

10. Look at everything as if it is a gift, because it is. Be thankful

for the things you have, no matter how small. Someday you will

realize how blessed you were. Be thankful now.

This is enough to start with. Please do these things, all of them.

This is what you can do for me. Thank you, friends. Sorry for long

post. Sometimes this is the only thing that helps me.

#mustardseed #Love #Live

Chapter 23

The next piece of writing I would like to share with you is a poem I wrote a couple of years before I was diagnosed with cancer. I didn't know then how much I would cling to this verse. I didn't know then how God would use me to reach people with this message. I didn't know it, but God did. It was His plan all along.

This poem is about the Mustard Seed and Matthew 17:20.

Matthew 17:20 "Truly I tell you, if you have faith as small as a mustard seed, you can say to this mountain, 'Move from here to there', and it will move. Nothing will be impossible for you."

Why the Mustard Seed?

When I was a young girl, I noticed something in our living room.

Something that had probably always been there,

But on this day, it caught my attention.

A necklace of some sort, hanging out of a Bible in our living room.

It was beautiful, and I knew it was something special.

When I asked my mom about it, she told me that it had been Grandma McGuire's.

When my mother was little, her grandmother had told her about the mustard seed....and about how the seed was so tiny,

But it grew into something very great.

She explained this to me, and I didn't really get it.

How could something so small be so great.

This verse makes sense to me more and more... and is one that I find comfort in.

Especially when my faith is lacking.

Some days, my faith is so strong that it can carry me and others. Other times, I feel I need to be carried.

This verse comforts me, as I know that even when my faith is small, it is still powerful.

I hope this verse, and others, will bless you and bring you comfort as well.

Andrea

Chapter 24

I don't know what the future holds, none of us do. No one is promised tomorrow. Time and people are precious. But I do know who holds tomorrow. I know where I'm going next. I know that God still has me here for a reason. I'm not done here. There is much more to do. I am thankful He is giving me today, and allowing me to share this book, His book. For as long as He will let me, I will sing and praise His name. He is still telling me to Trust Him. And so I do.

What is your mountain? God wants to help you move it. Maybe you have more than one. Maybe there are mountains all around you! Allow Him to work in your life. Make those mountains move!